Bologna Sandwich, Ballet Slippers, and other B.S.

Bologna Sandwich, Ballet Slippers, and other B.S.

by

Q Dogg

ISBN: 1-58721-274-9

About the Book

B.S. was written during my adolescent years. So, a lot of it may be offensive to some people. *B.S.* should be taken as a funny, humorous book.

POEMS

<u>Cheesecake</u>

You see it staring at you through the glass
Although you're overweight and you got a fat ass

With a forklift, you're easily motivated
And your largest clothes are skin-tight
The sign says it's low fat
But anyhow, you grunt at the sight

You enter and sit
After walking all day, you smell like shit

The waiter approaches, you're using the table as a sling
You say cheesecake, he asks, "One piece, or the whole thing?"

You get your piece, and it's gone in a flash
You reach into your purse and grab some more cash

After pieces two and three, you start number four
As soon as it's gone, you beg for more

No more cheesecake, you ate it all
Your belt's about to snap, and to the floor your belly will fall

After you leave, you walk down the street
Then your heart stops and falls to your feet

You lie on the ground and begin to shake
This never would have happened if you had only one piece of cheesecake

Doughnuts

Most doughnuts are made in a deep-fryer
Some people fill them with weed to get much higher

Some are glazed, some are not
Some are baked, or filled with pot

Doughnuts are good any time of day
They're even better than curds and whey

Doughnuts are better when they're dunked
Dip them in beer to get drunk

Don't like doughnuts? So you say
Well, guess what, you're dumb and gay

Buy them fresh and not day-old
'Cause they will be green and covered with mold

When you dunk, use coffee, milk, or even pop
But be careful, don't let it drop

Doughnuts are round and sometimes square
You can eat them here or you can eat them there

If doughnuts become illegal, you'll have to be sly as a fox
To get your greedy hands on a big fat box

My father said, with a twinkle in his eye
"I'll eat doughnuts 'til the day that I die"
That next day, he was found dead on the floor
In his left hand a doughnut, in his right some more

What are those voices I hear everywhere?
The lost souls of doughnuts in the air
Their cries had been once forgotten

Now they're all crusty and rotten
The human that left them uneaten
Should be tracked down and brutally beaten

Covered with chocolate, filled with cream
Pinch me now, it must be a dream

Doughnuts are given too much power
Doughnuts every minute, doughnuts every hour

Doughnuts are inquisitly symmetrical
Their aero-dynamics are a spectacle

My favorite doughnuts are round
In a box, on a table is where they're found

This poem sucks, and so do I
I'm gonna go eat some doughnuts, so see ya later, bye bye

Gangsta Love

I remember when we's first met
I was wearing speedos an' you was all wet

Did we meet at the bank? No!
'Twas da swap meet, stank ho

I do everythang just ta please ya
Even though yo a crusty skeeza

When we git's on with da smoochie-smoochie
I know dat yo my triflin' hoochie

I like you, an' yo nappy fro
I like you, ya nuppy ho

It's gangsta love, so here's da pitch
You'll always be my gangsta bitch

I Like

I like a sandwich that's made from squid
I like to shave horses with cousin Sid

I like to eat Chinese at Mexican-type places
I like to bet on horses at the Greyhound races

I like driving steamrollers, in winter, for their good traction
I like watching the Spanish Channel with closed caption

I like it when green means stop and red means go
I like making sand castles in the snow

I like Novocain, it gets me numb and nummer
I like to shovel the driveway in the middle of summer

I like decaf when it's caffinated
I like PG movies when they're X rated

I like lifting cars, they're light as a feather
I like running through the sprinkler in winter weather

I like to wear Versace when I clean the bathroom
I like to use the lawnmower when I vacuum

I like to tickle people's feet when they wear shoes
I like it when the cow barks and the dog moos

I Saw A Rich Lady

I saw a rich lady
She had big land with a big house
I saw a rich lady
She fed big cheese to a big mouse

I saw a rich lady
She had big keys to a big car
I saw a rich lady
She smoked big amounts of big cigars

I saw a rich lady
She had a big boss at her big job
I saw a rich lady
She supported a big man, a very big slob

I saw a rich lady
She had a big yard with big blades of grass
I saw a rich lady
She ate big meals to enlarge her big fat ass

I Wish I Was A Dildo

I wish I was a dildo
I'd get pussy, and I'd get it a lot
If I get used often
I'd be all sweaty and hot

If I was a dildo, I could be myself
I wouldn't have to worry about looks and personality
I wouldn't have to worry about size or nationality

I wish I was a dildo
I'd get pussy, and I'd get it a lot
It would be a big hairy chick
Who definitely wouldn't be hot

I wish I was a dildo
She'd be a smelly, ugly ho
That doesn't sound very good to me
I'm glad I'm not a dildo

Ice Cream

Ice cream is cool
And that's not a figure of speech
I cannot choose the kind I want
I guess I'll take one of each

I like ice cream best when it is cold
It's even better when covered with mold

I like to put ice cream in my socks
And let it squish between my toes
I like to put it in my ears
And shove it up my nose

I like ice cream on a cone
I even called it on the telephone
I would speak, but it wouldn't talk back
So I ate the mother fucker, and that was the end of that

Six Times A Day

I can remember when
We were back on the farm bailing hay
We did it six times a day

I can remember when
We would go to the park to play
We did it six times a day

I can remember when
My dog would run stray
He did it six times a day

I can remember when
My two best friends told me they were gay
They did it six times a day

The Ant

One of the wold's smallest creatures
Never studied by the greatest teachers

Many legs, but not a single arm
It wouldn't hurt a fly, or deliver harm

I befriended an ant one sunny day
On my pretzel crumbs, he was munching away

His life ended quickly, and out of the blue
'Cause that little bastard met the bottom of my shoe

The Good Stuff..........2-Ply

It's best when it's white
But don't wad it up too tight
And sometimes for weirdoes at night
It gives them great fright
But it always comes out all right

It's a whole lot better than lickin'
And is better than using a rubber chicken

I wouldn't recommend a decoy duck
When it's gone, you're out of luck
So, please don't use a hockey puck
Because it is small and will not work
And people will call you a dumbass jerk

If and when you do run out, don't cry
This never would have happened if you used 2-ply

So next time you need to scrape 'er
Use only the good toilet paper

The Tree

I sway here, to and fro
with this rope around my neck
From a bet I lost a few days ago
It seemed harmless, so what the heck

I look at the ground
A few inches below my feet
If I don't die from suffocation
I will die from the heat

I wonder if I will live another day
I wonder if I will find that back-stabbing cheater
I wonder what I will do when I see him
I wonder if I paid the parking meter

3 Parts

I Met A Man

I met a man
When I was walking down the street
He said he just got out of prison
And his nick-name there was fresh-meat

I met a man
At the grocery store
He was a pimp from Long Beach
So I bought the food pyramid and a $50 whore

I met a man
When I was "sittin' on the can"
He asked if I had a gerbil he could borrow
I said, "Fuck you man!"

I Met A Chimp

I met a chimp
At the state zoo
He said I looked like a monkey
I said he looked like one too

I met a chimp
When I was buying a pair of shoes
He said he just won the lottery
And wanted to take me on a cruise

I met a chimp
At the bar, he had a frown
He said people picked on him
For being the only ape in monkey town

I Met A Girl

I met a girl
On the Hollywood Walk of Fame
After we had sex seven times
I asked her what was her name

I met a girl
When I was digging through the trash
I got her to have sex with me
Because I said my wife died in a plane crash

I met a girl
After the war
I gave her 50 bucks
And we had sex on the floor

LISTS

Nice Additives To A Bathroom

Vending Machines

Folding Chairs (for when you have an audience)

Pictures of shaved farm animals

Windows on every wall

Strobe light

Vibrating soap-on-a-rope

Peppermint toilet paper

Voice activated toilet flushing

Fun house mirrors

Remote control toilet seats

Ways To Tell If Your Car Is A Piece Of Crap

The only time the heater works is in summer, and the only time the A/C works is in Winter.

You get in an accident, but your car looks the same as before.

All the windows are 20% duct tape and 80% plastic.

Your brakes don't lock up, but you don't have ABS.

For better traction, you take off the normal tires and put on the tires from your Mountain bike.

Your car won't start in below zero temperatures.

Someone cuts the brake lines, but you don't notice any difference.

Your door key and ignition key consist of a crowbar and a screwdriver.

The only thing your car has in common with a Lamborghini is gas mileage.

Best Names For Characters In A Movie

Justin Case (just in case)

John Q. Public (self explanatory)

Elemeno Pecueres (LMNOPQRS)

Richard Ked (dick head)

Jack Pot (jackpot)

Mickey Deez (McDonalds)

Hue Janis (huge anus)

Difficult Decisions For Young People To Make

Cut the grass or smoke grass

Take dance lessons or sumo wrestling

Get a job or get pregnant

Say no to drugs or say yes to selling drugs

Get into a fight at school or start a fight at school

Ride your bike or carjack

<u>Ways To Get Fired From Your Job</u>

If you are a postal worker, blow away people with your Semi-Automatic AK 47.

If you are Mexican, it doesn't matter. You can get a job anywhere when you work for $0.28 an hour.

If you are a business owner, piss off a customer, then they come back with a sawed-off and blow your fuckin' head off. Well, then you are not fired, you're terminated.

If you are a garbage man, steal everybody's trashcans and build a castle with them. Then run around naked, with your underwear over your head.

If you are a janitor, mop a floor and then don't put out the "WET FLOOR" sign, and then laugh your balls off when stupid kids fall and break their leg, and then sue the school, which goes bankrupt, and then you're collecting welfare trying to support a wife and three kids.

If you are a dog catcher, at the end of the day, take all the dogs to a cheap motel and have sex with them.

<u>Ways To Tell If You Are Getting Old</u>

You have wood glue, glue for paper, a hot glue gun, and glue for your teeth.

When you have conversations, the word you use the most is "What?".

You spend most of your social security on cheap perfume.

From your neck to your ankles, you can't tell if it's your front or back.

Alternative Titles For Gilligan's Island

Skipper's Island

Whitey's Island

Trapped On An Island With People You Hardly Know And All There Is To Eat Is Coconuts.

Good Times (whitey style)

The Little Minnow That Could

The Millionaire And His Wife........ And Gilligan, Skipper, The Movie Star, The Professor And Mary Ann.

Gilligan's Little Dingy Mishap

God Alterations For The 90's

Old God Name	New God Name	Background
Poseidon	Westsiden	son of a gangsta god and his bitch god of the West Coast
Zeus	Juice	son of Gin and Juice god of Kickin' It
Aphrodite	Asshole Whitey	son of Mr. and Mrs. Charlie god of Rednecks
Apollo	A Pillow	Juice's brother god of Hangovers
Nike	Dike	sister to Juice and A Pillow goddess of Lesbians
Hades	Rabies	son of Herpes and Syphilis god of Getting Bit In The Ass By A Dog
Ares	Hairweaves	daughter of Rogaine goddess of Nappy 'Fros
Athena	Awiena	son of Scrotum god of Masculinity
Hephaustus	Asbestos	son of Biohazard god of Hazardous Waste

<u>New Ice Cream Flavors</u>

spinach
rice cake
nacho
mud
pickle
penicillin
head lice
liver
sperm whale
dirty old sock
JD
cough drop
cheeseburger
monkey brains
Drano
crabs
toe nail
used condom
cottage cheese
Rogaine

Indian Names

Yusalotta TP

Big Dancing Snake

Hairy Beaver

Wakes With A Woodie

Bangalotta Chickies
(these two are brothers)
Bangalotta Girlies

*Stands With A Stiffie

Isamajor Druggie

*I heard this one from D, I don't know where he got it from.

Little Jimmy's X-Mas List

A Helmet

T & A

Gift Certificates to Jiffy Lube

Large box of small condoms

Cherry Pie

A raincoat

Shaft (the movie)

Dick Spanky's instruction manual on <u>How To Box The Clown</u>

Six pack (triplets)

Ways To Tell If Someone Just Hit A Landmark Birthday

Someone who just turned 16 would be seen driving a rusty, old, piece of junk car.

Someone who just turned 18 buys cigarettes for no reason, and becomes a compulsive gambler.

Someone who just turned 65 goes out and gets all the discounts and free stuff they can get.

Someone who just turned 21 orders a "triple-double" at a bar.

Someone who just turned 5 ½ will boast repeatedly that they are almost 6.

Ways To Tell If You Are A Party Animal

Every morning, when you wake up, you don't know whose house you're in.

When you brush your teeth, you think the spearmint toothpaste tastes like beer.

By the time you wake up, you realize that you are late for the next party.

Most people have a beer can collection, you have a keg collection.

When you got your first flask, you couldn't remember your initials, so it reads "E&J".

When you use the phrase, "Me an' the boys", you are referring to Jack Daniels, Johnny Walker, and Captain Morgan.

The liquor store phone number is your first speed dial number on your telephone.

Redneck Games

pin the tail on the cousin

"pick your toes" races

sell your blood for money to buy a pack of smokes

shoe string and fishing hook rock climbing

take a crap on the ceiling

find a matching pair of socks

shut off the lights, and find the broken floor board

shaved chicken races

who can pick the most lint from their bellybuttons

hide an' go sleep (with your sister)

<u>Sexual Football League</u>

Green Bay Fudge Packers

San Francisco Forty Giners (or 69ers)

St. Louis Rams

Washington Pink Skins

Atlanta Failcums

Oakland Panty Raiders

Pittsburgh Feelers

Carolina Pant Hards

Buffalo Dills

Tampa Bay Fuck-in-rears

Minnesota BiQueens

Dallas Gayboys

Names For A "Sex" Store

Slippey's

Wacky World

Bump & Grind

Hearty Handshake

Jimmy Lube

Grease Monkey

Toys R Us

Hardees

People Who Should've Been Gangsta Rappers
(and their first hit song)

Uncle Ben ....Rice, Rice, Baby

Mr. T ....I Pity Da Foo, When I Cap His Ass

Aunt Jemima ....It Was A Good Breakfast

Boyz II Men ....Crying Our Way, Straight Out Of Compton

Barry White ....Can't Get Enough Of Your Ass, Babe

Martin Luther King Jr. ....I Have A Dream, Westsiiiiide!

Mike Tyson ....I De-Eared His Mother Fuckin' Ass

Evander Holyfield ....Ouch! Don't De-Ear My Mother Fuckin' Ass

Ways To Tell If You Live In A Small Town

The cause of a traffic jam consists of a dead cow.

People combine the phrases "two-bit whore" and "one whore town" to come up with "two-bit whore town".

A new family moves into town and it doubles the population.

Livestock out-number people 2 to 1.

50% of the business' are motels and the other 50% are bars.

Strange Similarities

Opening a small package of crackers
Opening a condom package

Receiving E-Mail
Receiving your sentence (20? 40? Life?)

The feeling you get when listening to folk music
The feeling you get when you hug a tree

Playing "Tag" as a kid
Playing "Phone Tag" as an adult

Pin the tail on the donkey
Pin the number on the stock holder

Cruisin' around town, kickin' the bass
Cruisin' for a bruisin', getting kicked in the face

Jumping on a trampoline
Jumping on a slutty whore

Making a porno
Making a home video

Selling your blood to buy drugs
Selling your drugs to buy drugs

Things A Girl Will Say To Talk A Guy Out Of Sex

You remind me of my grandma.

Have you ever heard of female circumcisions?

That Mexican guy, who sells hotdogs on the street, is a good kisser.

Get off me, I don't even know you!

What was your name again?

Hey, I thought you were my cousin!

What does your sister look for in a girl?

Have you ever met my husband?

Ways To Tell It's Too Hot Outside

The devil goes on vacation to a nice, warm, sunny place.

You use three air conditioners in one room.

Jack Frost goes to a nude beach.

Hell is a popular vacation spot.

For lunch, you have a steaming bowl of ice cream.

A cool, refreshing drink is a hot cup of coffee.

You drink ice cubes through a straw.

The only thing you wear is a really big hat.

Toughest Things To Say

(when said really, really fast)

Community Immunity

Telephone Cellophane

Worth The Wait Birth Date

Cinnamon Anonymous

M&M Enema

Possible Slogans For A Whore House

Come!

Come In!

Come Out!

You Can Come On The Rugs

You Got The Money, We Got The Honey

Breasts: So Good They Come In Pairs

We Put The "ho" In House

We Vacuum Our Whores Daily

Entrance In Rear

SONGS & RHYMES

Country Rap

My name is Farmer Bob an' I'm here to say
W'sup to my homie in Green Bay

I dusted a punk in my Chevy Truck
He thought he was tough so I showed him what's up

Bessy got sick from being under fed
I pulled out my AK and shot the fat cow in the head
Then we all had round steak
Sold Bessy's carcass for some money to make

Farmin' the fields on the Eastside
Picked up a bitch, yo, she wanted a ride
She wanted to fool around in the hay
I had to say, Today Was A Good Day

Droppin' On Heaven's Floor

(Formerly <u>Knockin' On Heaven's Door</u> by: Bob
Dylan)

Momma take this bong from me
I can't toke it any more
I'm getting stoned, too stoned to see
Feels like I'm droppin' on heaven's floor

Drop, drop, droppin' on heaven's floor
Drop, drop, droppin' on heaven's floor

Momma put my needles to the ground
I can't shoot them any more
That dope, whack cloud is coming down
Feels like droppin' on heaven's floor

Drop, drop, droppin' on heaven's floor
Drop, drop, droppin' on heaven's floor

Hillbilly Rap
(By: Slop Hoggy Hogg)

Ma is the missus and Pa is the mister
We marry our cousins, but I like my sister

We play with pigs and ride the steer
We only bathe about once a year

We play the banjo and our clothes don't fit
We can't read or write or do arithmetic

Ours clothes are dirty and we don't wear shoes
We're dumb as rocks and make our own booze

When there's nothing to eat, we pick our nose
When that's all gone, we pick our toes

When our kids act dumb, we tend to hit 'em
We get up with the chickens 'cause we sleep wit 'em

We see our relatives almost everywhere
We never shave or comb our hair

I Got You, Slave
(I Got You, Babe)

(Owner) They say you're dumb, but I don't know
   I won't find out until it shows

(Owner) Well, I don't know if all that's true
(Slave) 'Cause you own me and owner I hate you

Slave, I got you slave
   I got you slave

(Owner) I say you work, and don't pay rent
(Slave) I use old tools, that are all rusty and bent

(Owner) I guess that's so you don't have any rights
(Slave) I'd go to jail if we got into a fight

Slave, I got you slave
   I got you slave

(Slave) I pick cotton in the spring
(Owner) When I hit you, your head will ring

(Slave) And when I'm sad, and I frown
(Slave) You beat me up then beat me down

(Owner) Let them say the day's too long
(Slave) I don't care, 'cause I'm black and strong

(Owner) I whip your back, time after time
(Owner) It may hurt you, but I feel fine

Slave, I got you slave
   I got you slave

(Owner) I got you for the rest of your life

83

(Slave)   I got you to sell my wife

(Owner) I got you to cut my grass
(Slave)   I got you to kick my ass

(Owner) I got you, you never put up a fight
(Slave)   I got you to beat me day and night

(Owner) I got you and I won't let go
(Owner) Because I got you in a sleeper hold

Slave, I got you slave
       I got you slave
       I got you slave
       I got you slave

I Wanna Potpie
(I Wanna Get High by: Cypress Hill)

I wanna potpie, potpie
I wanna potpie, potpie

Well that's the chickenlastic
Crust I've twisted
To slamify, foodify, punk on your pie tin

Go get the chicken
You don't know whatcha missin'
Catch a bird and another bird, finger lickin'

Yes I roast and fry
Chicken off the roadside
A road side, the good side
To the hungry ones who eat potpies

For the hungry, who get the munchies
The veggies are good 'cause they ain't crunchy
What's with the luncheon, yo I'm not jokin' around
People learnin' about what they munchin'

My oven's on high when I cook the gravy
Tell Bill Clinton to go and pick daisies
X-raysies
Macys
When I see the crust rise
I wanna pot pie, potpie
I wanna pot pie, potpie

<u>* Jack and Jill</u>

Jack and Jill
Went up the hill
To get it on
Jack was smilin'
'Cause he was gonna drop the bomb

He hurt Jill
And she started to cry
'Cause he left the bitch
He was dope, fly

*This isn't that good. I wrote it in three minutes to win a bet.

<u>Jingle Bells</u>

Dashing out the way
Of the low-ride Chevrolet
Over the trashcans I go
As he pulls out his AK

My nine was in my hand
My finger on the trigger
He's claiming this his land
What a stupid nigga

Oh, jingle bells, what the hell?
I blew that punk away
Oh what fun it is to blast
Punk mutha fuckaz all day

I shot him in the head
So now that fuckers dead
I do not have to worry
Until I go to bed

So now I'm on the street
Just like a nigga in heat
Some guy starts some shit
So I knock him off his feet

Oh, jingle bells, what the hell?
I blew that punk away
Oh what fun it is to blast
Punk mutha fuckaz all day

Being followed by a cop
This I cannot stop
So I turned around, and broke his neck
This I cannot top

I just killed The Man
So now I need a plan
To get out of here
I could live in Japan

Oh, jingle bells, what the hell?
I blew that punk away
Oh what fun it is to blast
Punk mutha fuckaz all day

Peter, Peter, Monkey-Beater

Peter, Peter, monkey-beater
Had a wife, but couldn't eat her
He put her out with a shotgun shell
Then screwed her sister and screwed her well

Silencer
(Formerly <u>Silent Night</u>)

Silencer
Pull the trigger
Blown away
Wit da AK
Round yon hole in his brain
Throw his body into a lake
Sleep In heavenly peace
Sleep in heavenly peace

The Old Woman In The Hood

There was an old woman
Who lived in the hood
She had so many children an'
Ain't none of them no good
She gave them all chitlin'
Without any heat
She smacked them all silly
An' sent them to the swapmeet

STORY

The Ding-Dong Adventure

In the times of dinosaurs, they ate plants and flesh. But, this story has nothing to do with dinosaurs. Today, we eat unhealthy crap that is killing off the human race. This is a story about a snack who made his way to the top and took a tragic fall.

Sure there were Twinkies, Ho-Hos, Oreos, and Oatmeal Cream Pies; but, no one was filled with cream like the Ding-Dong. Everyone favored the Twinkie. They loved the yellow cake with the delicious, creamy frosting inside. Ho-Hos had their spot in the sun too; frosted chocolate cake rolled up with chocolate frosting "drooled" all over it. All people liked to twist an Oreo and lick the sweet, white nectar inside, then dunk it in milk. Oatmeal Cream Pies were made from oatmeal, so nobody cares. But, they were filled with cream.

As you can tell, Ding-Dong had a lot of competition. He tried and tried, but was falling behind. People would ignore his cries of, "Pick me, I taste better than all the others." But people were used to the others. They always choose Twinkie or Ho-Ho, then walk down the isle and pick up Oreo. All hope was lost, until one night Ding-Dong was drinking his problems away in a bar. Still sober, he saw Ho-Ho celebrating his great sales of the day. After he had five too many, Ding-Dong dragged him out into the street and beat the crap out of him. That made Ding-Dong feel a lot better.

The next day, Ding-Dong had a lot of confidence. He even did better in sales. He decided to celebrate by going to a dance club. Ding-Dong showed up the same time as Oreo. Oreo insulted Ding-Dong's Ford Pinto, which was rejected by valet parking. Ding-Dong was pissed, so he keyed Oreo's brand new Ferrari F355 before he went in. Later that night, when Oreo left, he saw what happened and became emotionally scarred.

The next day, Oreo's sales dropped while Ding-Dong's continued to rise. To reward himself, Ding-Dong bought a new car. Actually, he bought a Durango. The next day, he showed up for work in style. Oatmeal Cream Pie was mocking Ding-Dong for his sudden success and the fact that Ding-Dong's sales were much lower than his own. On his break, Ding-Dong took care of business. He called his buddies Mike and Ike. They "fixed" Oatmeal Cream Pie's car. After work, Oatmeal Cream Pie started his car and it instantly exploded. He was lucky enough to survive the "accident", but he had to miss many months of work.

Now, the only one left was Twinkie. Ding-Dong was catching up fast to the "yellow sponge". It was only a matter of days until Ding-Dong broke even with Twinkie. One night, Twinkie was taking a stroll, when he noticed he was being followed by a bunch of Raisenettes. And as we all know, Raisenettes stick together; so they all attacked Twinkie. It was Twinkie's lucky coincidence that Ding-Dong was walking by. Ding-Dong pulled out his Nine and busted a cap in every Raisenette. Twinkie said Ding-Dong could have anything for helping him. Ding-Dong said, "I want all the power you had." And with that, he capped Twinkie seven times.

Weeks and months went by. Twinkie and Oatmeal Cream Pie were still in the hospital. Oreo and Ho-Ho have not mentally recovered yet. And Ding-Dong was powerful. He had connections with the president, congress, and the Mafia. He was in the big bucks and had all the glory. Not too much later, Twinkie recovered, Oatmeal Cream Pie was working again, and Ho-Ho and Oreo were in the right state of mind. They all feared Ding-Dong because of his power. They feared him so much that they hired a hit man to take him out. The hit man succeeded.

Seventeen years passed, when out of the blue came Ding-Dong. The other four were shocked. Ding-Dong explained that he is actually the son of the first Ding-Dong. So the new Ding-Dong made a deal with Twinkie, Oatmeal Cream Pie, Oreo, and Ho-Ho. They all decided to share the power and share all sales. All of them became wealthy, powerful friends.

About the Author

Q Dogg is the Whitest, Black, Asian, Mexican American on earth. Brought up in the mid-upper area of a huge small city in the most northern southwest eastern part of the U.S., Q. Dogg holds his dignity high. He makes every attempt to be hated by the haters and liked by the likers. His advice, "Don't be a hater."